Thomas Bailey Aldrich

The Sisters' Tragedy, with Other Poems, Lyrical and Dramatic

Thomas Bailey Aldrich

The Sisters' Tragedy, with Other Poems, Lyrical and Dramatic

ISBN/EAN: 9783744770330

Printed in Europe, USA, Canada, Australia, Japan

Cover: Foto ©ninafisch / pixelio.de

More available books at **www.hansebooks.com**

THE SISTERS' TRAGEDY WITH OTHER POEMS, LYRICAL AND DRAMATIC. BY THOMAS BAILEY ALDRICH

BOSTON AND NEW YORK
HOUGHTON, MIFFLIN AND
COMPANY. MDCCCXCI

The Riverside Press, Cambridge, Mass., U S. A.
Electrotyped and Printed by H. O. Houghton & Company

THE SISTERS' TRAGEDY

ETC.

CONTENTS

THE SISTERS' TRAGEDY

THE SISTERS' TRAGEDY

A. D. 1670

AGLÄE, a widow.
MURIEL, her unmarried sister.

IT happened once, in that brave land that lies

For half the twelvemonth wrapt in sombre skies,

Two sisters loved one man.   He being dead,

Grief loosed the lips of her he had not wed,

And all the passion that through heavy years

Had masked in smiles unmasked itself in tears.

No purer love may mortals know than this,

The hidden love that guards another's bliss.

High in a turret's westward-facing room,

Whose painted window held the sunset's bloom,

The two together grieving, each to each

Unveiled her soul with sobs and broken speech.

Both still were young, in life's rich summer yet ;

And one was dark, with tints of violet

In hair and eyes, and one was blond as she

Who rose — a second daybreak — from the sea,

Gold-tressed and azure-eyed.   In that lone place,

Like dusk and dawn, they sat there face to face.

She spoke the first whose strangely silvering hair

No wreath had worn, nor widow's weed might wear,

And told her blameless love, and knew no shame —

Her holy love that, like a vestal flame

Beside the sacred body of some queen

Within a guarded crypt, had burned unseen

From weary year to year.   And she who heard

Smiled proudly through her tears and said no word,

But, drawing closer, on the troubled brow

Laid one long kiss, and that was words enow !

MURIEL.

Be still, my heart !   Grown patient with thine ache,

Thou shouldst be dumb, yet needs must speak, or break.

The world is empty now that he is gone.

AGLÄE.

Ay, sweetheart !

MURIEL.

None was like him, no, not one.

From other men he stood apart, alone

In honor spotless as unfallen snow.

Nothing all evil was it his to know ;

His charity still found some germ, some spark

Of light in natures that seemed wholly dark.

He read men's souls ; the lowly and the high

Moved on the self-same level in his eye.

Gracious to all, to none subservient,

Without offence he spake the word he meant —

His word no trick of tact or courtly art,

But the white flowering of the noble heart.

Careless he was of much the world counts gain,

Careless of self, too simple to be vain,

Yet strung so finely that for conscience-sake

He would have gone like Cranmer to the stake.

I saw — how could I help but love ?   And you —

AGLÄE.

At this perfection did I worship too . . .

'T was this that stabbed me.   Heed not what I say !

I meant it not, my wits are gone astray,

With all that is and has been.   No, I lie —

Had he been less perfection, happier I !

MURIEL.

Strange words and wild !   'T is the distracted mind

Breathes them, not you, and I no meaning find.

AGLÄE.

Yet 't were as plain as writing on a scroll

Had you but eyes to read within my soul. —

How a grief hidden feeds on its own mood,

Poisons the healthful currents of the blood

With bitterness, and turns the heart to stone !

I think, in truth, 't were better to make moan,

And so be done with it.   This many a year,

Sweetheart, have I laughed lightly and made cheer,

Pierced through with sorrow !

                Then the widowed one

With sorrowfullest eyes beneath the sun,

Faltered, irresolute, and bending low

Her head, half whispered,

                Dear, how could you know ?

What masks are faces ! — yours, unread by me

These seven long summers ; mine, so placidly

Shielding my woe !   No tremble of the lip,

No cheek's quick pallor let our secret slip !

Mere players we, and she that played the queen,

Now in her homespun, looks how poor and mean !

How shall I say it, how find words to tell

What thing it was for me made earth a hell

That else had been my heaven!   'T would blanch your
     cheek

Were I to speak it.   Nay, but I will speak,

Since like two souls at compt we seem to stand,

Where nothing may be hidden.   Hold my hand,

But look not at me!   Noble 't was, and meet,

To hide your heart, nor fling it at his feet

To lie despised there.   Thus saved you our pride

And that white honor for which earls have died.

You were not all unhappy, loving so!

I with a difference wore my weight of woe.

My lord was he.   It was my cruel lot,

My hell, to love him — for he loved me not!

Then came a silence.   Suddenly like death

The truth flashed on them, and each held her breath —

A flash of light whereby they both were slain,

She that was loved and she that loved in vain!

THE LAST CÆSAR

1851–1870

I

Now there was one who came in later days

To play at Emperor: in the dead of night

Stole crown and sceptre, and stood forth to light

In sudden purple.   The dawn's straggling rays

Showed Paris fettered, murmuring in amaze,

With red hands at her throat — a piteous sight.

Then the new Cæsar, stricken with affright

At his own daring, shrunk from public gaze

In the Elysée, and had lost the day

But that around him flocked his birds of prey,

Sharp-beaked, voracious, hungry for the deed.

'Twixt hope and fear behold great Cæsar hang !

Meanwhile, methinks, a ghostly laughter rang

Through the rotunda of the Invalides.

II

What if the boulevards, at set of sun,

Reddened, but not with sunset's kindly glow ?

What if from quai and square the murmured woe

Swept heavenward, pleadingly ?   The prize was won,

A kingling made and Liberty undone.

No Emperor, this, like him awhile ago,

But his Name's shadow ; that one struck the blow

Himself, and sighted the street-sweeping gun !

This was a man of tortuous heart and brain,

So warped he knew not his own point of view —

The master of a dark, mysterious smile.

And there he plotted, by the storied Seine

And in the fairy gardens of St. Cloud,

The Sphinx that puzzled Europe, for awhile.

III

I see him as men saw him once — a face

Of true Napoleon pallor ; round the eyes

The wrinkled care ; mustache spread pinion-wise,

Pointing his smile with odd sardonic grace

As wearily he turns him in his place,

And bends before the hoarse Parisian cries—

Then vanishes, with glitter of gold-lace

And trumpets blaring to the patient skies.

Not thus he vanished later !   On his path

The Furies waited for the hour and man,

Foreknowing that they waited not in vain.

Then fell the day, O day of dreadful wrath !

Bow down in shame, O crimson-girt Sedan !

Weep, fair Alsace! weep, loveliest Lorraine !

So mused I, sitting underneath the trees

In that old garden of the Tuileries,

Watching the dust of twilight sifting down

Through chestnut boughs just toucht with autumn's

brown —

Not twilight yet, but that illusive bloom

Which holds before the deep-etched shadows come ;

For still the garden stood in golden mist,

Still, like a river of molten amethyst,

The Seine slipt through its spans of fretted stone,

And, near the grille that once fenced in a throne,

The fountains still unbraided to the day

The unsubstantial silver of their spray.

A spot to dream in, love in, waste one's hours !

Temples and palaces, and gilded towers,

And fairy terraces ! — and yet, and yet

Here in her woe came Marie Antoinette,

Came sweet Corday, Du Barry with shrill cry,

Not learning from her betters how to die !

Here, while the Nations watched with bated breath,

Was held the saturnalia of Red Death !

For where that slim Egyptian shaft uplifts

Its point to catch the dawn's and sunset's drifts

Of various gold, the busy Headsman stood. . . .

Place de la Concorde — no, the Place of Blood !

And all so peaceful now !   One cannot bring

Imagination to accept the thing.

Lies, all of it ! some dreamer's wild romance —

High-hearted, witty, laughter-loving France !

In whose brain was it that the legend grew

Of Mænads shrieking in this avenue,

Of watch-fires burning, Famine standing guard,

Of long-speared Uhlans in that palace-yard !

What ruder sound this soft air ever smote

Than a bird's twitter or a bugle's note ?

What darker crimson ever splashed these walks

Than that of rose-leaves dropping from the stalks ?

And yet — what means that charred and broken wall,

That sculptured marble, splintered, like to fall,

Looming among the trees there ? . . . And you say

This happened, as it were, but yesterday ?

And here the Commune stretched a barricade,

And there the final desperate stand was made ?

Such things have been ?   How all things change and
      fade !

How little lasts in this brave world below !

Love dies ; hate cools ; the Cæsars come and go ;

Gaunt Hunger fattens, and the weak grow strong.

Even Republics are not here for long !

Ah, who can tell what hour may bring the doom,

The lighted torch, the tocsin's heavy boom !

IN WESTMINSTER ABBEY

" The Southern Transept. hardly known by any other name but Poets' Corner."

DEAN STANLEY.

TREAD softly here ; the sacredest of tombs

Are those that hold your Poets.   Kings and queens

Are facile accidents of Time and Chance.

Chance sets them on the heights, they climb not there !

But he who from the darkling mass of men

Is on the wing of heavenly thought upborne

To finer ether, and becomes a voice

For all the voiceless, God anointed him :

His name shall be a star, his grave a shrine.

Tread softly here, in silent reverence tread.

Beneath those marble cenotaphs and urns

Lies richer dust than ever nature hid

Packed in the mountain's adamantine heart,

Or slyly wrapt in unsuspected sand —

The dross men toil for, and oft stain the soul.

How vain and all ignoble seems that greed

To him who stands in this dim claustral air

With these most sacred ashes at his feet !

This dust was Chaucer, Spenser, Dryden this —

The spark that once illumed it lingers still.

O ever-hallowed spot of English earth !

If the unleashed and happy spirit of man

Have option to revisit our dull globe,

What august Shades at midnight here convene

In the miraculous sessions of the moon,

When the great pulse of London faintly throbs,

And one by one the stars in heaven pale !

ALEC YEATON'S SON

GLOUCESTER, AUGUST, 1720

THE wind it wailed, the wind it moaned,

And the white caps flecked the sea;

" An' I would to God," the skipper groaned,

"I had not my boy with me!"

Snug in the stern-sheets, little John

Laughed as the scud swept by;

But the skipper's sunburnt cheek grew wan

As he watched the wicked sky.

"Would he were at his mother's side!"

And the skipper's eyes were dim.

"Good Lord in heaven, if ill betide,

What would become of him!

"For me — my muscles are as steel,

For me let hap what may ;

I might make shift upon the keel

Until the break o' day.

"But he, he is so weak and small,

So young, scarce learned to stand —

O pitying Father of us all,

I trust him in Thy hand !

"For Thou, who markest from on high

A sparrow's fall — each one ! —

Surely, O Lord, thou 'lt have an eye

On Alec Yeaton's son ! "

Then, helm hard-port ; right straight he sailed

Towards the headland light :

The wind it moaned, the wind it wailed,

And black, black fell the night.

Then burst a storm to make one quail

 Though housed from winds and waves —

They who could tell about that gale

 Must rise from watery graves !

Sudden it came, as sudden went ;

 Ere half the night was sped,

The winds were hushed, the waves were spent,

 And the stars shone overhead.

Now, as the morning mist grew thin,

 The folk on Gloucester shore

Saw a little figure floating in

 Secure, on a broken oar !

Up rose the cry, " A wreck ! a wreck !

 Pull, mates, and waste no breath ! " —

They knew it, though 't was but a speck

 Upon the edge of death !

Long did they marvel in the town
　At God his strange decree,
That let the stalwart skipper drown
　And the little child go free !

AT THE FUNERAL OF A MINOR POET

[One of the Bearers soliloquizes :]

. . . Room in your heart for him, O Mother Earth,

Who loved each flower and leaf that made you fair,

And sang your praise in verses manifold

And delicate, with here and there a line

From end to end in blossom like a bough

The May breathes on, so rich it was.   Some thought

The workmanship more costly than the thing

Moulded or carved, as in those ornaments

Found at Mycæne.   And yet Nature's self

Works in this wise ; upon a blade of grass,

Or what small note she lends the woodland thrush,

 Lavishing endless patience.   He was born

Artist, not artisan, which some few saw

And many dreamed not.   As he wrote no odes

When Crœsus wedded or Mæcenas died,

And gave no breath to civic feasts and shows,

He missed the glare that gilds more facile men —

A twilight poet, groping quite alone,

Belated, in a sphere where every nest

Is emptied of its music and its wings.

Not great his gift; yet we can poorly spare

Even his slight perfection in an age

Of limping triolets and tame rondeaux.

He had at least ideals, though unreached,

And heard, far off, immortal harmonies,

Such as fall coldly on our ear to-day.

The mighty Zolaistic Movement now

Engrosses us — a miasmatic breath

Blown from the slums.   We paint life as it is,

The hideous side of it, with careful pains,

Making a god of the dull Commonplace.

For have we not the old gods overthrown

And set up strangest idols ?   We would clip

Imagination's wing and kill delight,

Our sole art being to leave nothing out

That renders art offensive.   Not for us

Madonnas leaning from their starry thrones

Ineffable, nor any heaven-wrought dream

Of sculptor or of poet ; we prefer

Such nightmare visions as in morbid brains

Take shape and substance, thoughts that taint the air

And make all life unlovely.   Will it last ?

Beauty alone endures from age to age,

From age to age endures, handmaid of God.

Poets who walk with her on earth go hence

Bearing a talisman.   You bury one,

With his hushed music, in some Potter's Field ;

The snows and rains blot out his very name,

As he from life seems blotted : through Time's glass

Slip the invisible and magic sands

That mark the century, then falls a day

The world is suddenly conscious of a flower,

Imperishable, ever to be prized,

Sprung from the mould of a forgotten grave.

'T is said the seeds wrapt up among the balms

And hieroglyphics of Egyptian kings

Hold strange vitality, and, planted, grow

After the lapse of thrice a thousand years.

Some day, perchance, some unregarded note

Of our poor friend here — some sweet minor chord

That failed to lure our more accustomed ear —

May witch the fancy of an unborn age.

Who knows, since seeds have such tenacity?

Meanwhile he 's dead, with scantiest laurel won

And little of our Nineteenth Century gold.

So, take him, Earth, and this his mortal part,

With that shrewd alchemy thou hast, transmute

To flower and leaf in thine unending Springs!

BATUSCHKA.[1]

FROM yonder gilded minaret

Beside the steel-blue Neva set,

I faintly catch, from time to time,

The sweet, aerial midnight chime —

    "God save the Tsar!"

Above the ravelins and the moats

Of the white citadel it floats;

And men in dungeons far beneath

Listen, and pray, and gnash their teeth —

    "God save the Tsar!"

The soft reiterations sweep

Across the horror of their sleep,

---

[1] "Little Father," or "Dear Little Father," a term of endearment applied to the Tsar in Russian folk-song.

As if some dæmon in his glee

Were mocking at their misery —

    " God save the Tsar ! "

In his Red Palace over there,

Wakeful, he needs must hear the prayer.

How can it drown the broken cries

Wrung from his children's agonies? —

    " God save the Tsar ! "

Father they called him from of old —

Batuschka ! . . . How his heart is cold !

Wait till a million scourgëd men

Rise in their awful might, and then —

    God save the Tsar !

ACT V

[Midnight.]

FIRST, two white arms that held him very close,

And ever closer as he drew him back

Reluctantly, the loose gold-colored hair

A thousand delicate fibres reaching out

Still to detain him; then some twenty steps

Of iron staircase winding round and down,

And ending in a narrow gallery hung

With Gobelin tapestries — Andromeda

Rescued by Perseus, and the sleek Diana

With her nymphs bathing; at the farther end

A door that gave upon a starlit grove

Of citron and clipt palm-trees; then a path

As bleached as moonlight, with the shadow of leaves

Stamped black upon it; next a vine-clad length

Of solid masonry ; and last of all

A Gothic archway packed with night, and then —

A sudden gleaming dagger through his heart.

TENNYSON

I

SHAKESPEARE and Milton — what third blazoned name

　Shall lips of after-ages link to these?

　His who, beside the wild encircling seas,

Was England's voice, her voice with one acclaim,

For threescore years; whose word of praise was fame,

　Whose scorn gave pause to man's iniquities.

II

What strain was his in that Crimean war?

　A bugle-call in battle; a low breath,

　Plaintive and sweet, above the fields of death!

So year by year the music rolled afar,

From Euxine wastes to flowery Kandahar,

　Bearing the laurel or the cypress wreath.

III

Others shall have their little space of time,

    Their proper niche and bust, then fade away

    Into the darkness, poets of a day ;

But thou, O builder of enduring rhyme,

Thou shalt not pass !   Thy fame in every clime

    On earth shall live where Saxon speech has sway.

IV

Waft me this verse across the winter sea,

    Through light and dark, through mist and blinding
       sleet,

    O winter winds, and lay it at his feet ;

Though the poor gift betray my poverty,

At his feet lay it : it may chance that he

    Will find no gift, where reverence is, unmeet.

THE SHIPMAN'S TALE

LISTEN, my masters! I speak naught but truth.

From dawn to dawn they drifted on and on,

Not knowing whither nor to what dark end.

Now the North froze them, now the hot South scorched.

Some called to God, and found great comfort so ;

Some gnashed their teeth with curses, and some laughed

An empty laughter, seeing they yet lived,

So sweet was breath between their foolish lips.

Day after day the same relentless sun,

Night after night the same unpitying stars.

At intervals fierce lightnings tore the clouds,

Showing vast hollow spaces, and the sleet

Hissed, and the torrents of the sky were loosed.

From time to time a hand relaxed its grip,

And some pale wretch slid down into the dark

With stifled moan, and transient horror seized

The rest who waited, knowing what must be.

At every turn strange shapes reached up and clutched

The whirling wreck, held on awhile, and then

Slipt back into that blackness whence they came.

Ah, hapless folk, to be so tost and torn,

So racked by hunger, fever, fire, and wave,

And swept at last into the nameless void —

Frail girls, strong men, and mothers with their babes!

And was none saved?

My masters, not a soul!

O shipman, woful, woful is thy tale!

Our hearts are heavy and our eyes are dimmed.

What ship is this that suffered such ill fate?

What ship, my masters?   Know ye not? — The World!

"I VEX ME NOT WITH BROODING ON THE YEARS"

I VEX me not with brooding on the years
   That were ere I drew breath : why should I then
   Distrust the darkness that may fall again
   When life is done?   Perchance in other spheres —
Dead planets — I once tasted mortal tears,
   And walked as now among a throng of men,
   Pondering things that lay beyond my ken,
   Questioning death, and solacing my fears.
Ofttimes indeed strange sense have I of this,
   Vague memories that hold me with a spell,
   Touches of unseen lips upon my brow,
Breathing some incommunicable bliss!
   In years foregone, O Soul, was all not well?
   Still lovelier life awaits thee.   Fear not thou!

MONODY ON THE DEATH OF WENDELL PHILLIPS

ONE by one they go

Into the unknown dark —

Star-lit brows of the brave,

Voices that drew men's souls.

Rich is the land, O Death !

Can give you dead like our dead ! —

Such as he from whose hand

The magic web of romance

Slipt, and the art was lost !

Such as he who erewhile —

The last of the Titan brood —

With his thunder the Senate shook ;

Or he who, beside the Charles,

Untoucht of envy or hate,

Tranced the world with his song ;

Or that other, that grey-eyed seer

Who in pastoral Concord ways

With Plato and Hâfiz walked.

II

Not of these was the man

Whose wraith, through the mists of night,

Through the shuddering wintry stars,

Has passed to eternal morn.

Fit were the moan of the sea

And the clashing of cloud on cloud

For the passing of that soul !

Ever he faced the storm !

No weaver of rare romance,

No patient framer of laws,

No maker of wondrous rhyme,

No bookman wrapt in his dream.

His was the voice that rang

In the fight like a bugle-call,

And yet could be tender and low

As when, on a night in June,

The hushed wind sobs in the pines.

His was the eye that flashed

With a sabre's azure gleam,

Pointing to heights unwon !

III

Not for him were these days

Of clerkly and sluggish calm —

To the petrel the swooping gale !

Austere he seemed, but the hearts

Of all men beat in his breast ;

No fetter but galled his wrist,

No wrong that was not his own.

What if those eloquent lips

Curled with the old-time scorn ?

What if in needless hours

His quick hand closed on the hilt ?

'T was the smoke from the well-won fields

That clouded the veteran's eyes.

A fighter this to the end !

Ah, if in coming times

Some giant evil arise,

And Honor falter and pale,

His were a name to conjure with !

God send his like again !

INTERLUDES

INTERLUDES

ECHO–SONG

I

WHO can say where Echo dwells ?

  In some mountain-cave, methinks,

  Where the white owl sits and blinks ;

Or in deep sequestered dells,

Where the foxglove hangs its bells,

     Echo dwells.

      Echo !

       Echo !

II

Phantom of the crystal Air,

  Daughter of sweet Mystery !

  Here is one has need of thee ;

Lead him to thy secret lair,

Myrtle brings he for thy hair —

Hear his prayer,

Echo !

Echo !

III

Echo, lift thy drowsy head,

And repeat each charmëd word

Thou must needs have overheard

Yestere'en ere, rosy-red,

Daphne down the valley fled —

Words unsaid,

Echo !

Echo !

IV

Breathe the vows she since denies !

She hath broken every vow ;

What she would she would not now —

Thou didst hear her perjuries.

Whisper, whilst I shut my eyes,

Those sweet lies,

Echo!

Echo!

A MOOD

A BLIGHT, a gloom, I know not what, has crept upon my
gladness —

Some vague, remote ancestral touch of sorrow, or of mad-
ness;

A fear that is not fear, a pain that has not pain's insistence;

A sense of longing, or of loss, in some foregone exist-
ence;

A subtle hurt that never pen has writ nor tongue has
spoken —

Such hurt perchance as Nature feels when a blossomed
bough is broken.

GUILIELMUS REX

The folk who lived in Shakespeare's day
And saw that gentle figure pass
By London Bridge, his frequent way —
They little knew what man he was.

The pointed beard, the courteous mien,
The equal port to high and low,
All this they saw or might have seen —
But not the light behind the brow!

The doublet's modest gray or brown,
The slender sword-hilt's plain device,
What sign had these for prince or clown?
Few turned, or none, to scan him twice.

Yet 't was the king of England's kings !

The rest with all their pomps and trains

Are mouldered, half-remembered things —

'T is he alone that lives and reigns !

"PILLARED ARCH AND SCULPTURED TOWER"

PILLARED arch and sculptured tower

Of Ilium have had their hour;

The dust of many a king is blown

On the winds from zone to zone;

Many a warrior sleeps unknown.

Time and Death hold each in thrall,

Yet is Love the lord of all;

Still does Helen's beauty stir

Because a poet sang of her!

THRENODY

I

Upon your hearse this flower I lay.

Brief be your sleep! You shall be known

When lesser men have had their day:

Fame blossoms where true seed is sown,

Or soon or late, let Time wrong what it may.

II

Unvext by any dream of fame,

You smiled, and bade the world pass by:

But I — I turned, and saw a name

Shaping itself against the sky —

White star that rose amid the battle's flame!

III

Brief be your sleep, for I would see

Your laurels — ah, how trivial now

To him must earthly laurel be

Who wears the amaranth on his brow !

How vain the voices of mortality !

SESTET

SENT TO A FRIEND WITH A VOLUME OF TENNYSON

WOULDST know the clash of knightly steel on steel?

Or list the throstle singing loud and clear?

Or walk at twilight by some haunted mere

In Surrey; or in throbbing London feel

Life's pulse at highest — hark, the minster's peal! . . .

Turn but the page, that various world is here!

A TOUCH OF NATURE

WHEN first the crocus thrusts its point of gold

Up though the still snow-drifted garden mould,

And folded green things in dim woods unclose

Their crinkled spears, a sudden tremor goes

Into my veins and makes me kith and kin

To every wild-born thing that thrills and blows.

Sitting beside this crumbling sea-coal fire,

Here in the city's ceaseless roar and din,

Far from the brambly paths I used to know,

Far from the rustling brooks that slip and shine

Where the Neponset alders take their glow,

I share the tremulous sense of bud and briar

And inarticulate ardors of the vine.

MEMORY

My mind lets go a thousand things,

Like dates of wars and deaths of kings,

And yet recalls the very hour —

'T was noon by yonder village tower,

And on the last blue noon in May —

The wind came briskly up this way,

Crisping the brook beside the road ;

Then, pausing here, set down its load

Of pine-scents, and shook listlessly

Two petals from that wild-rose tree.

"I'LL NOT CONFER WITH SORROW"

I 'LL not confer with Sorrow
    Till to-morrow;
But Joy shall have her way
    This very day.

Ho, eglantine and cresses
    For her tresses ! —
Let Care, the beggar, wait
    Outside the gate.

Tears if you will — but after
    Mirth and laughter;
Then, folded hands on breast
    And endless rest.

A DEDICATION

Take these rhymes into thy grace,
Since they are of thy begetting,
Lady, that dost make each place
Where thou art a jewel's setting.

Some such glamour lend this Book:
Let it be thy poet's wages
That henceforth thy gracious look
Lies reflected on its pages.

NO SONGS IN WINTER

THE sky is gray as gray may be,

There is no bird upon the bough,

There is no leaf on vine or tree.

In the Neponset marshes now

Willow-stems, rosy in the wind,

Shiver with hidden sense of snow.

So too 't is winter in my mind,

No light-winged fancy comes and stays:

A season churlish and unkind.

Slow creep the hours, slow creep the days,

The black ink crusts upon the pen —

Just wait till bluebirds, wrens, and jays

And golden orioles come again!

"LIKE CRUSOE, WALKING BY THE LONELY STRAND"

Like Crusoe, walking by the lonely strand

And seeing a human footprint on the sand,

Have I this day been startled, finding here,

Set in brown mould and delicately clear,

Spring's footprint — the first crocus of the year!

O sweet invasion!   Farewell solitude!

Soon shall wild creatures of the field and wood

Flock from all sides with much ado and stir,

And make of me most willing prisoner!

THE LETTER

EDWARD ROWLAND SILL, DIED FEBRUARY 27, 1887

I HELD his letter in my hand,
    And even while I read
The lightning flashed across the land
    The word that he was dead.

How strange it seemed! His living voice
    Was speaking from the page
Those courteous phrases, tersely choice,
    Light-hearted, witty, sage.

I wondered what it was that died!
    The man himself was here,
His modesty, his scholar's pride,
    His soul serene and clear.

These neither death nor time shall dim,

Still this sad thing must be —

Henceforth I may not speak to him,

Though he can speak to me!

SARGENT'S PORTRAIT OF EDWIN BOOTH
AT "THE PLAYERS"

THAT face which no man ever saw

And from his memory banished quite,

With eyes in which are Hamlet's awe

And Cardinal Richelieu's subtle light,

Looks from this frame.   A master's hand

Has set the master-player here,

In the fair temple that he planned

Not for himself.   To us most dear

This image of him !   "It was thus

He looked ; such pallor touched his cheek ;

With that same grace he greeted us —

Nay, 't is the man, could it but speak ! "

Sad words that shall be said some day —

Far fall the day !   O cruel Time,

Whose breath sweeps mortal things away,

Spare long this image of his prime,

That others standing in the place

Where, save as ghosts, we come no more,

May know what sweet majestic face

The gentle Prince of Players wore !

PAULINE PAVLOVNA

PAULINE PAVLOVNA

SCENE: *St. Petersburg. Period: the present time. A ballroom in the winter palace of the Prince——. The ladies in character costumes and masks. The gentlemen in official dress and unmasked, with the exception of six tall figures in scarlet kaftans, who are treated with marked distinction as they move here and there among the promenaders. Quadrille music throughout the dialogue.*
Count SERGIUS PAVLOVICH PANSHINE, *who has just arrived, is standing anxiously in the doorway of an antechamber with his eyes fixed upon a lady in the costume of a maid of honor in the time of Catherine II. The lady presently disengages herself from the crowd, and passes near Count* PANSHINE, *who impulsively takes her by the hand and leads her across the threshold of the inner apartment, which is unoccupied.*

HE.

Pauline !

SHE.

You knew me ?

HE.

How could I have failed ?

A mask may hide your features, not your soul.

There is an air about you like the air

That folds a star.   A blind man knows the night,

And feels the constellations.   No coarse sense

Of eye or ear had made you plain to me.

Through these I had not found you ; for your eyes,

As blue as violets of our Novgorod,

Look black behind your mask there, and your voice —

I had not known that either.   My heart said,

" Pauline Pavlovna."

SHE.

Ah !   Your heart said that ?

You trust your heart, then !   'T is a serious risk ! —

How is it you and others wear no mask ?

HE.

The Emperor's orders.

SHE.

Is the Emperor here ?

I have not seen him.

HE.

He is one of the six

In scarlet kaftans and all masked alike.

Watch — you will note how every one bows down

Before those figures, thinking each by chance

May be the Tsar ; yet none knows which is he.

Even his counterparts are left in doubt.

Unhappy Russia !   No serf ever wore

Such chains as gall our Emperor these sad days.

He dare trust no man.

SHE.

All men are so false.

HE.

Spare one, Pauline Pavlovna.

SHE.

No ; all, all !

I think there is no truth left in the world,

In man or woman.   Once were noble souls. —

Count Sergius, is Nastasia here to-night?

HE.

Ah! then you know!   I thought to tell you first.

Not here, beneath these hundred curious eyes,

In all this glare of light ; but in some place

Where I could throw me at your feet and weep.

In what shape came the story to your ear?

Decked in the teller's colors, I 'll be sworn ;

The truth, but in the livery of a lie,

And so must wrong me.   Only this is true :

The Tsar, because I risked my wretched life

To shield a life as wretched as my own,

Bestows upon me, as supreme reward —

O irony! — the hand of this poor girl.

Says, *Here, I have the pearl of pearls for you,*

Such as was never plucked from out the deep

By Indian diver, for a Sultan's crown.

Your joy 's decreed, and stabs me with a smile.

SHE.

And she — she loves you?

HE.

                I know not, indeed.

Likes me, perhaps.   What matters it? — *her* love!

The guardian, Sidor Yurievich, consents,

And she consents.   No love in it at all,

A mere caprice, a young girl's spring-tide dream.

Sick of her ear-rings, weary of her mare,

She 'll have a lover — something ready-made,

Or improvised between two cups of tea —

A lover by imperial ukase!

Fate said her word — I chanced to be the man!

If that grenade the crazy student threw

Had not spared me, as well as spared the Tsar,

All this would not have happened.   I 'd have been

A hero, but quite safe from her romance.

She takes me for a hero — think of that!

Now by our holy Lady of Kazan,

When I have finished pitying myself,

I 'll pity her.

SHE.

Oh no ; begin with her ;

She needs it most.

HE.

At her door lies the blame.

Whatever falls.   She, with a single word,

With half a tear, had stopt it at the first,

This cruel juggling with poor human hearts.

SHE.

The Tsar commanded it — you said the Tsar.

HE.

The Tsar does what she wills — God fathoms why.

Were she his mistress, now ! but there 's no snow

Whiter within the bosom of a cloud,

Nor colder either.   She is very haughty,

For all her fragile air of gentleness ;

With something vital in her, like those flowers

That on our desolate steppes outlast the year.

Resembles you in some things.   It was that

First made us friends.   I do her justice, see !

For we were friends in that smooth surface way

We Russians have imported out of France.

Alas ! from what a blue and tranquil heaven

This bolt fell on me !   After these two years,

My suit with Ossip Leminoff at end,

The old wrong righted, the estates restored,

And my promotion, with the ink not dry !

Those fairies which neglected me at birth

Seemed now to lavish all good gifts on me —

Gold roubles, office, sudden dearest friends.

The whole world smiled ; then, as I stooped to taste

The sweetest cup, freak dashed it from my lip.

This very night — just think, this very night —

I planned to come and beg of you the alms

I dared not ask for in my poverty.

I thought me poor then.   How stript am I now!

There's not a ragged mendicant one meets

Along the Nevski Prospekt but has leave

To tell his love, and I have not that right!

Pauline Pavlovna, why do you stand there

Stark as a statue, with no word to say?

SHE.

Because this thing has frozen up my heart.

I think that there is something killed in me,

A dream that would have mocked all other bliss.

What shall I say?   What would you have me say?

HE.

If it be possible, the word of words!

SHE, *very slowly.*

Well, then — I love you.   I may tell you so

This once, . . . and then forever hold my peace.

We cannot stay here longer unobserved.

No — do not touch me! but stand further off,

And seem to laugh, as if we jested — eyes,

Eyes everywhere! Now turn your face away . . .

I love you.

HE.

With such music in my ears

I would death found me. It were sweet to die

Listening! You love me — prove it.

SHE.

Prove it — how?

I prove it saying it. How else?

HE.

Pauline,

I have three things to choose from ; you shall choose :

This marriage, or Siberia, or France.

The first means hell ; the second, purgatory ;

The third — with you — were nothing less than heaven !

SHE, *starting.*

How dared you even dream it !

HE.

I was mad.

This business has touched me in the brain.

Have patience ! the calamity 's so new.

(*Pauses.*)

There is a fourth way ; but that gate is shut

To brave men who hold life a thing of God.

SHE.

Yourself spoke there ; the rest was not of you.

HE.

Oh, lift me to your level !   So I 'm safe.

What 's to be done ?

SHE.

There must be some path out.

Perhaps the Emperor —

HE.

Not a ray of hope !

His mind is set on this with that insistence

Which seems to seize on all match-making folk.

The fancy bites them, and they straight go mad.

SHE.

Your father's friend, the Metropolitan —

A word from him . . .

HE.

Alas, he too is bitten !

Gray-haired, gray-hearted, worldly wise, he sees

This marriage makes me the Tsar's protégé,

And opens every door to preference.

SHE.

Think while I think.   There surely is some key

Unlocks the labyrinth, could we but find it.

Nastasia !

HE.

What! beg life of her? Not I.

SHE.

Beg love.   She is a woman, young, perhaps

Untouched as yet of this too poisonous air.

Were she told all, would she not pity us?

For if she love you, as I think she must,

Would not some generous impulse stir in her,

Some latent, unsuspected spark illume?

How love thrills even commonest girl-clay,

Ennobling it an instant, if no more!

You said that she is proud; then touch her pride,

And turn her into marble with the touch.

But yet the gentler passion is the stronger.

Go to her, tell her, in some tenderest phrase

That will not hurt too much — ah, but 't will hurt! —

Just how your happiness lies in her hand

To make or mar for all time; hint, not say,

Your heart is gone from you, and you may find —

HE.

A casemate in St. Peter and St. Paul

For, say, a month ; then some Siberian town.

Not this way lies escape.   At my first word

That sluggish Tartar blood would turn to fire

In every vein.

SHE.

How blindly you read her,

Or any woman !   Yes, I know.   I grant

How small we often seem in our small world

Of trivial cares and narrow precedents —

Lacking that wide horizon stretched for men —

Capricious, spiteful, frightened. at a mouse ;

But when it comes to suffering mortal pangs,

The weakest of us measures pulse with you.

HE.

Yes, you, not she.   If she were at your height !

But there 's no martyr wrapt in *her* rose flesh.

There should have been ; for Nature gave you both

The self-same purple for your eyes and hair,

The self-same Southern music to your lips,

Fashioned you both, as 't were, in the same mould,

Yet failed to put the soul in one of you !

I know her wilful — her light head quite turned

In this court atmosphere of flatteries ;

A Moscow beauty, petted and spoiled there,

And since spoiled here ; as soft as swan's-down now,

With words like honey melting from the comb,

But being crossed, vindictive, cruel, cold.

I fancy her, between two rosy smiles,

Saying, " Poor fellow, in the Nertchinsk mines ! "

That is the sum of her.

SHE.

You know her not.

Count Sergius Pavlovich, you said no mask

Could hide the soul, yet how you have mistaken

The soul these two months — and the face to-night !

[*Removes her mask.*

HE.

You ! — it was *you !*

    .

SHE.

Count Sergius Pavlovich,

Go find Pauline Pavlovna — she is here —

And tell her that the Tsar has set you free.

[*She goes out hurriedly, replacing her mask.*

BAGATELLE

CORYDON

A PASTORAL

SCENE: *A roadside in Arcady.*

SHEPHERD.

GOOD sir, have you seen pass this way

A mischief straight from market-day?

You 'd know her at a glance, I think;

Her eyes are blue, her lips are pink;

She has a way of looking back

Over her shoulder, and, alack!

Who gets that look one time, good sir,

Has naught to do but follow her.

PILGRIM.

I have not seen this maid, methinks,

Though she that passed had lips like pinks.

SHEPHERD.

Or like two strawberries made one

By some sly trick of dew and sun.

PILGRIM.

A poet!

SHEPHERD.

Nay, a simple swain

That tends his flock on yonder plain,

Naught else, I swear by book and bell.

But she that passed — you marked her well.

Was she not smooth as any be

That dwell herein in Arcady?

PILGRIM.

Her skin was as the satin bark

Of birches.

SHEPHERD.

Light or dark?

PILGRIM.

Quite dark.

.

SHEPHERD.

Then 't was not she.

PILGRIM.

The peach's side

That 's next the sun is not so dyed

As was her cheek.   Her hair hung down

Like summer twilight falling brown ;

And when the breeze swept by, I wist

Her face was in a sombre mist.

SHEPHERD.

No, that is not the maid I seek.

Her hair lies gold against the cheek ;

Her yellow tresses take the morn

Like silken tassels of the corn.

And yet — brown locks are far from bad.

PILGRIM.

Now I bethink me, this one had

A figure like the willow-tree

Which, slight and supple, wondrously

Inclines to droop with pensive grace,

And still retains its proper place ;

A foot so arched and very small

The marvel was she walked at all ;

Her hand — in sooth I lack for words —

Her hand, five slender snow-white birds.

Her voice — though she but said " God-speed " —

Was melody blown through a reed ;

The girl Pan changed into a pipe

Had not a note so full and ripe.

And then her eye — my lad, her eye !

Discreet, inviting, candid, shy,

An outward ice, an inward fire,

And lashes to the heart's desire —

Soft fringes blacker than the sloe.

SHEPHERD, *thoughtfully.*

Good sir, which way did *this* one go?

.   .   .   .

PILGRIM, *solus.*

So, he is off!   The silly youth

Knoweth not Love in sober sooth.

He loves — thus lads at first are blind —

No woman, only Womankind.

I needs must laugh, for, by the Mass,

No maid at all did this way pass!

AT A READING

THE spare Professor, grave and bald,

Began his paper.   It was called,

I think, " A Brief Historic Glance

At Russia, Germany, and France."

A glance, but to my best belief

'T was almost anything but brief —

A wide survey, in which the earth

Was seen before mankind had birth ;

Strange monsters basked them in the sun,

Behemoth, armored glyptodon,

And in the dawn's unpractised ray

The transient dodo winged its way ;

Then, by degrees, through silt and slough,

We reached Berlin — I don't know how.

The good Professor's monotone

Had turned me into senseless stone

Instanter, but that near me sat

Hypatia in her new spring hat,

Blue-eyed, intent, with lips whose bloom

Lighted the heavy-curtained room.

Hypatia — ah, what lovely things

Are fashioned out of eighteen springs !

At first, in sums of this amount,

The eighteen winters do not count.

Just as my eyes were growing dim

With heaviness, I saw that slim,

Erect, elastic figure there,

Like a pond-lily taking air.

She looked so fresh, so wise, so neat,

So altogether crisp and sweet,

I quite forgot what Bismarck said,

And why the Emperor shook his head,

And how it was Von Moltke's frown

Cost France another frontier town.

The only facts I took away

From the Professor's theme that day

Were these : a forehead broad and low,

Such as the antique sculptures show ;

A chin to Greek perfection true ;

Eyes of Astarte's tender blue ;

A high complexion without fleck

Or flaw, and curls about her neck.

THE MENU

I BEG you come to-night and dine.

A welcome waits you, and sound wine —

The Roederer chilly to a charm,

As Juno's breath the claret warm,

The sherry of an ancient brand.

No Persian pomp, you understand —

A soup, a fish, two meats, and then

A salad fit for aldermen

(When aldermen, alas, the days !

Were really worth their *mayonnaise*) ;

A dish of grapes whose clusters won

Their bronze in Carolinian sun ;

Next, cheese — for you the Neufchâtel,

A bit of Cheshire likes me well ;

Café au lait or coffee black,

With Kirsch or Kümmel or Cognac

(The German band in Irving Place

By this time purple in the face) ;

Cigars and pipes.   These being through,

Friends shall drop in, a very few —

Shakespeare and Milton, and no more.

When these are guests I bolt the door,

With Not at Home to any one

Excepting Alfred Tennyson.

AN ELECTIVE COURSE

LINES FOUND AMONG THE PAPERS OF A HARVARD UNDER-

GRADUATE

THE bloom that lies on Fanny's cheek

Is all my Latin, all my Greek ;

The only sciences I know

Are frowns that gloom and smiles that glow ;

Siberia and Italy

Lie in her sweet geography ;

No scholarship have I but such

As teaches me to love her much.

Why should I strive to read the skies,

Who know the midnight of her eyes ?

Why should I go so very far

To learn what heavenly bodies are !

Not Berenice's starry hair

With Fanny's tresses can compare;

Not Venus on a cloudless night,

Enslaving Science with her light,

Ever reveals so much as when

She stares and droops her lids again.

If Nature's secrets are forbidden

To mortals, she may keep them hidden.

Æons and æons we progressed

And did not let that break our rest;

Little we cared if Mars o'erhead

Were or were not inhabited;

Without the aid of Saturn's rings

Fair girls were wived in those far springs;

Warm lips met ours and conquered us

Or ere thou wert, Copernicus!

Graybeards, who seek to bridge the chasm

'Twixt man to-day and protoplasm,

Who theorize and probe and gape,

And finally evolve an ape —

Yours is a harmless sort of cult,

If you are pleased with the result.

Some folks admit, with cynic grace,

That you have rather proved your case.

These dogmatists are so severe !

Enough for me that Fanny 's here,

Enough that, having long survived

Pre-Eveic forms, she *has* arrived —

An illustration the completest

Of the survival of the sweetest.

Linnæus, avaunt !   I only care

To know what flower she wants to wear.

I leave it to the addle-pated

To guess how pinks originated,

As if it mattered !   The chief thing

Is that we have them in the Spring,

And Fanny likes them.   When they come,

I straightway send and purchase some.

The Origin of Plants — go to !

Their proper end *I* have in view.

O loveliest book that ever man

Looked into since the world began

Is Woman !   As I turn those pages,

As fresh as in the primal ages,

As day by day I scan, perplext,

The ever subtly changing text,

I feel that I am slowly growing

To think no other work worth knowing.

And in my copy — there is none

So perfect as the one I own —

I find no thing set down but such

As teaches me to love it much.

L'EAU DORMANTE

CURLED up and sitting on her feet,

   Within the window's deep embrasure,

Is Lydia ; and across the street,

   A lad, with eyes of roguish azure,

Watches her buried in her book.

In vain he tries to win a look,

And from the trellis over there

Blows sundry kisses through the air,

Which miss the mark, and fall unseen,

Uncared for.   Lydia is thirteen.

My lad, if you, without abuse,

   Will take advice from one who 's wiser,

And put his wisdom to more use

   Than ever yet did your adviser ;

If you will let, as none will do,

Another's heartbreak serve for two,

You 'll have a care, some four years hence,

How you lounge there by yonder fence

And blow those kisses through that screen —

For Lydia will be seventeen.

THALIA

A MIDDLE-AGED LYRICAL POET IS SUPPOSED TO BE TAKING FINAL LEAVE OF THE MUSE OF COMEDY. SHE HAS BROUGHT HIM HIS HAT AND GLOVES, AND IS ABSTRACTEDLY PICKING A THREAD OF GOLD HAIR FROM HIS COAT SLEEVE AS HE BEGINS TO SPEAK:

I SAY it under the rose —

    oh, thanks! — yes, under the laurel,

We part lovers, not foes;

    we are not going to quarrel.

We have too long been friends

    on foot and in gilded coaches,

Now that the whole thing ends,

    to spoil our kiss with reproaches.

I leave you; my soul is wrung;

    I pause, look back from the portal —

Ah, I no more am young,

    and you, child, you are immortal !

Mine is the glacier's way,

    yours is the blossom's weather —

When were December and May

    known to be happy together ?

Before my kisses grow tame,

    before my moodiness grieve you,

While yet my heart is flame,

    and I all lover, I leave you.

So, in the coming time,

    when you count the rich years over,

Think of me in my prime,

    and not as a white-haired lover,

Fretful, pierced with regret,

    the wraith of a dead Desire

Thrumming a cracked spinet

    by a slowly dying fire.

When, at last, I am cold —

    years hence, if the gods so will it —

Say, " He was true as gold,"

    and wear a rose in your fillet !

Others, tender as I,

    will come and sue for caresses,

Woo you, win you, and die —

    mind you, a rose in your tresses !

Some Melpomene woo,

    some hold Clio the nearest ;

You, sweet Comedy — you

    were ever sweetest and dearest !

Nay, it is time to go —

    when writing your tragic sister

Say to that child of woe

how sorry I was I missed her.

Really, I cannot stay,

though "parting is such sweet sorrow" . . .

Perhaps I will, on my way

down-town, look in to-morrow!

PALINODE

WHO is Lydia, pray, and who

Is Hypatia? Softly, dear,

Let me breathe it in your ear —

They are you, and only you.

And those other nameless two

Walking in Arcadian air —

She that was so very fair?

She that had the twilight hair? —

They were you, dear, only you.

If I speak of night or day,

Grace of fern or bloom of grape,

Hanging cloud or fountain spray,

Gem or star or glistening dew,

Or of mythologic shape,

Psyche, Pyrrha, Daphne, say —

I mean you, dear, you, just you.

A PETITION

To spring belongs the violet, and the blown
Spice of the roses let the summer own.
Grant me this favor, Muse — all else withhold —
That I may not write verse when I am old.

And yet I pray you, Muse, delay the time!
Be not too ready to deny me rhyme;
And when the hour strikes, as it must, dear Muse,
I beg you very gently break the news.